D1505984

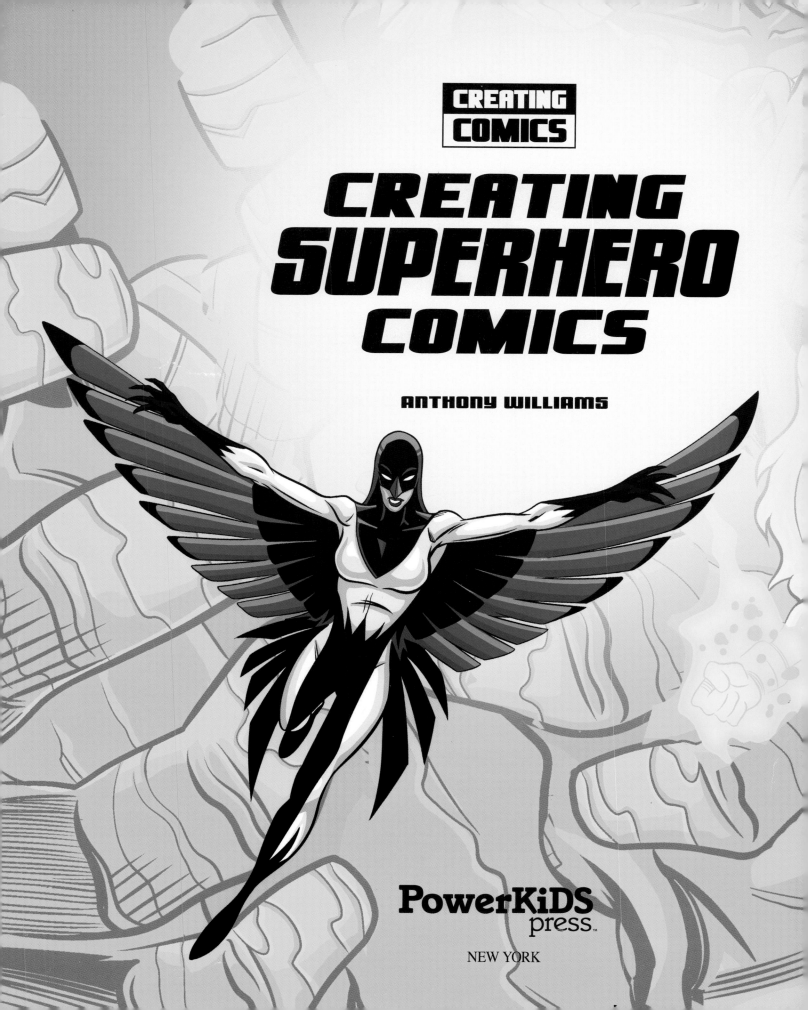

CREATING
COMICS

CREATING SUPERHERO COMICS

ANTHONY WILLIAMS

PowerKiDS
press™

NEW YORK

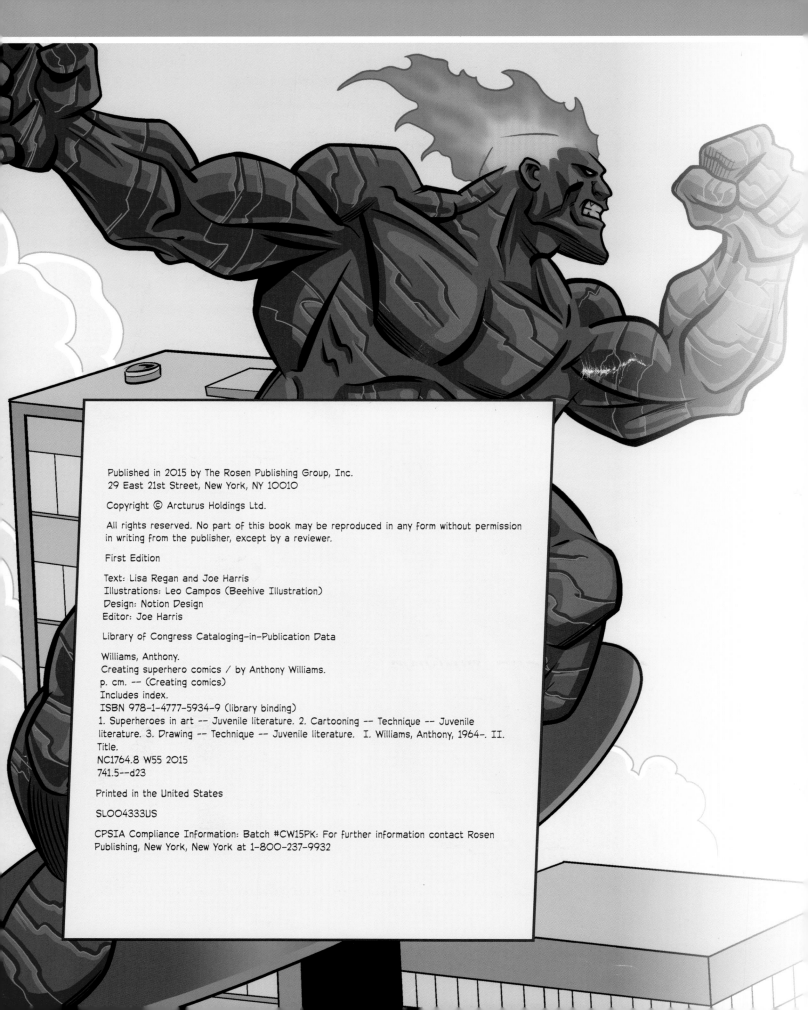

Published in 2015 by The Rosen Publishing Group, Inc.
29 East 21st Street, New York, NY 10010

First Edition

Text: Lisa Regan and Joe Harris
Illustrations: Leo Campos (Beehive Illustration)
Design: Notion Design
Editor: Joe Harris

Library of Congress Cataloging-in-Publication Data

Williams, Anthony.
Creating superhero comics / by Anthony Williams.
p. cm. -- (Creating comics)
Includes index.
ISBN 978-1-4777-5934-9 (library binding)
1. Superheroes in art -- Juvenile literature. 2. Cartooning -- Technique -- Juvenile literature. 3. Drawing -- Technique -- Juvenile literature. I. Williams, Anthony, 1964-. II. Title.
NC1764.8 W55 2015
741.5--d23

Printed in the United States

SL004333US

CPSIA Compliance Information: Batch #CW15PK: For further information contact Rosen Publishing, New York, New York at 1-800-237-9932

CONTENTS

TOOLS OF THE TRADE

YOU DON'T NEED EXPENSIVE EQUIPMENT TO START DRAWING SUPERHEROES. GATHER TOGETHER THE BASICS SHOWN HERE, AND THEN TAP INTO THE MOST IMPORTANT TOOL: IMAGINATION.

PENCILS

Soft (B, 2B) pencils are great for drawing loosely and are easy to erase. Fine point pencils are handy for adding detail.

ERASERS

A kneaded eraser molds to shape, so you can use it to remove pencil from tiny areas. Keep a clean, square-edged eraser to hand, too.

PENS

An artist's pens are his or her most precious tools! Gather a selection with different tips for varying the thickness of your line work.

FINE LINE AND BRUSH PENS

Fine line pens are excellent for small areas of detail. Brush pens are perfect for varying your line weight or shading large areas.

PENCILS, INKS, AND COLORS

HERE ARE THE FOUR MAIN STAGES OF CREATING A COLOR PICTURE. USE SCRAP PAPER WHILE YOU PRACTICE YOUR DRAWING, THEN WORK UP THE BEST POSES IN COLOR.

ROUGH SKETCHES

Start by making a rough sketch of your character. Work out their pose and proportions before adding any details.

TIGHT SKETCHES

When you are happy with the basic frame, you can tighten it up with firm pencil strokes, then add in some shading.

INKS

Finalize your line work by adding inks and erasing your pencil marks. Once the ink is dry, erase any guidelines still visible.

COLORS

If you are drawing the same characters many times, keep a note of what colors you use for their costumes and skin tone.

DRAWING HUMAN FIGURES

SUPERHEROES MAY HAVE BULKED-UP MUSCLES, BUT THEIR FRAMES ARE STILL BASED ON THE REAL HUMAN FORM. HERE ARE SOME RULES FOR BODY PROPORTIONS THAT YOU CAN USE AS A GUIDE WHEN DRAWING.

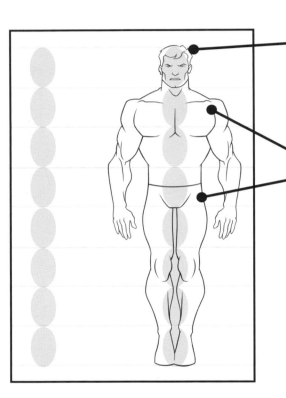

HEADS
The "head length" can be a useful measuring tool. A typical superhero character is about eight heads tall.

SHOULDERS AND HIPS
Generally, males are broadest at the shoulders while females are broadest at the hips. Superheroines sometimes break that rule.

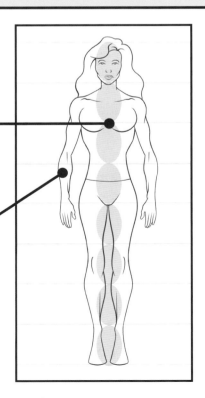

BODY AND LEGS
The average body measures three head lengths. The legs are at least four lengths.

ARMS
Arms end midthigh, between the hip and knee. Be careful not to give your characters overlong, apelike arms!

DRAWING HEADS

FOLLOW THESE SIMPLE GUIDELINES TO MAKE YOUR FACES LOOK REALISTIC. THIS WILL ALSO HELP WITH KEEPING FACES CONSISTENT FROM ONE PANEL TO THE NEXT.

EYES
Look in a mirror and you will see that your eyes are positioned about halfway down your face. The distance between the eyes is about one eye in width.

NOSE
The nostrils appear about halfway between the eyes and the chin. The sides of the nose at its widest point line up roughly with the inner corners of the eyes.

MOUTH
The mouth sits halfway between the nostrils and the chin.

EARS
The ears should extend from the top of the eyes to the bottom of the nose.

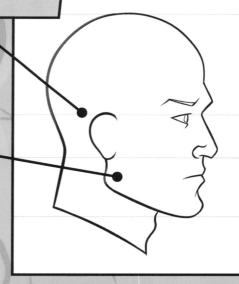

JAWLINES AND CHEEKBONES
Male superheroes tend to have a square jaw. Add finely chiseled cheekbones, and you have the classic heroic face shape.

FEMALE FACES
When drawing female characters, give them a more rounded jawline, thinner eyebrows, and a smaller nose. You can draw the outline of lips on female characters, but avoid this for male heroes ... or they will look like they are wearing lipstick.

G-FORCE
MASTER OF GRAVITY

ARE YOU READY TO DRAW YOUR FIRST SUPERHERO? ROCKET SCIENTIST TODD TRAVIS WAS BUILDING THE WARP DRIVE OF AN EXPERIMENTAL SHIP WHEN THE ENGINE EXPLODED. THE COSMIC ENERGY GAVE HIM THE ABILITY TO CONTROL GRAVITY. NOW HE FIGHTS CRIME ACROSS THE GALAXY!

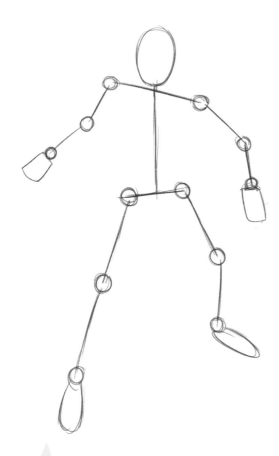

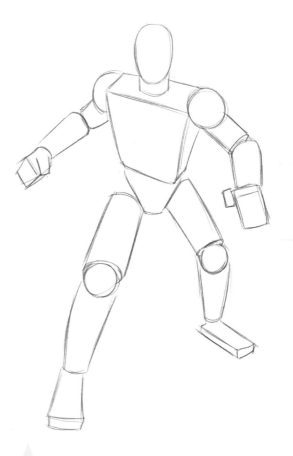

1 It's important that you get the initial pose and proportions right. Sketch a wireframe showing limbs and joints.

2 Use basic shapes to build on top of your wireframe. His hips are triangular, and his chest tapers to the waist. The leg that is closest to us looks slightly longer than the trailing leg.

3 Now you can bulk up the body and outline where the features will go. Sketch in G-Force's leg and arm muscles, and define those in his stomach area. Round off the joints and add details to the hands and feet, including fingers and knuckles.

4 It's costume time! What is your newly invented character going to look like? G-Force has some high-tech nodes across his chest and on his belt, which help him keep control of his gravity powers. His identity is hidden by a domino mask.

5 The inking stage is your opportunity to choose the strongest lines in your illustration and bring them out with nice, sharp line work. Keep your hand steady as you outline all those muscles. This cosmic hero is bulked-up *and* brainy, so bad guys had better beware!

6 When you're happy with your character, you can add color. Pick a bold blue and red. Use darker and paler tones for shadows and highlights. Classic superheroes tend to have primary colors—red, blue, and yellow—as their color palette.

STYLES OF SUPERHERO ART

THERE'S MORE THAN ONE WAY TO DRAW A SUPERHERO! DOC TWILIGHT HAS THE ABILITY TO CONTROL LIGHT AND DARKNESS ... AND HERE WE'VE DRAWN HIM WITH FOUR DIFFERENT APPROACHES.

MODERN SUPERHERO ART

Let's start with a modern take on our hero. Notice how the line work is light on the Doc's face, but it's heavier on his body. There are few large areas of ink. His face is very moody—he's almost grimacing!

ALL-ACTION STYLE

This "retro" art style harks back to the energetic line work of famous comic artist Jack Kirby. The lines on Doc Twilight's face and body are more angular—many of them are shaped like zigzags.

ANIMATED STYLE

In this "animated" style, the line work is much simpler. The detail is reduced in favor of clean, sweeping lines, but the proportions remain realistic. The shadows are turned into flat blocks of black ink.

NOIR STYLE

Noir is the French word for black. It's a style of artwork that tends to be used for stories about crime or the supernatural. It has large areas of shadow in place of fine details, with a strong contrast between colors.

VICTORY
THE ULTIMATE SOLDIER

LET'S CREATE ANOTHER SUPERHERO. SECRET MILITARY EXPERIMENTS HAVE TRANSFORMED FORMER MARINE VIKKI VENTURA—A.K.A. VICTORY—INTO A HUMAN FIGHTER PLANE. SHE CAN FLY AT SUPERSONIC SPEEDS AND FIRE BLASTS OF ENERGY FROM HER FINGERTIPS.

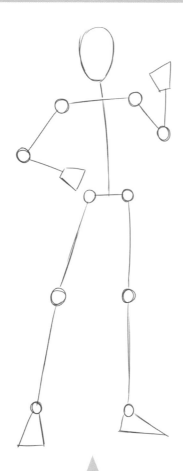

1 Sketch the wireframe with a line for the shoulders and slightly narrower hips. Her raised hand is her weapon.

2 Add the simple shapes that make up her body and limbs. Avoid using straight lines when you are drawing people. Slight curves give them more movement and poise.

3 Begin to add the details of her hair and face. Sketch your rough ideas for her costume, including wrist cuffs, belt, and boots. Add an outline of the power that she shoots from her clenched fist.

4 Use shading to define Victory's costume, including her short, armless jacket. Like many superheroes, her costume is tight-fitting and practical. Pay attention to the details of her winged chest symbol.

5 Is Victory fighting on the side of good or evil? You can use subtle details of her facial features to show her personality. We have carefully inked her face to show an open, friendly expression. However, if you lower her eyebrows, she will look more sinister.

6 The bold tones of Victory's outfit contrast well with the energy glow around her hand, making the image more dramatic. She looks relaxed but confident, and her functional, no-frills jacket shows her down-to-earth side. Move over ... there's a new hero in town!

CREATING NEW CHARACTERS

IF YOU'RE CREATING YOUR OWN SUPERHERO COMIC, YOU MIGHT WANT TO USE YOUR OWN SUPERHEROES OR SUPERVILLAINS. WHERE CAN YOU FIND INSPIRATION FOR NEW CHARACTERS?

ANIMAL HEROES

One way to devise a new character is to take inspiration from an animal. Many superheroes, such as Batman and Spider-Man, have the characteristics and capabilities of animals.

Magpie is a brilliant thief. Like real magpies, she has a love of shiny things—such as priceless jewels!

NATURE HEROES

You can take your starting point from other aspects of nature, such as clouds, rainbows, volcanoes, or plants.

Tanglevine's body is covered in tough, thorny armor. He can use the vines sprouting from his back to entangle his enemies.

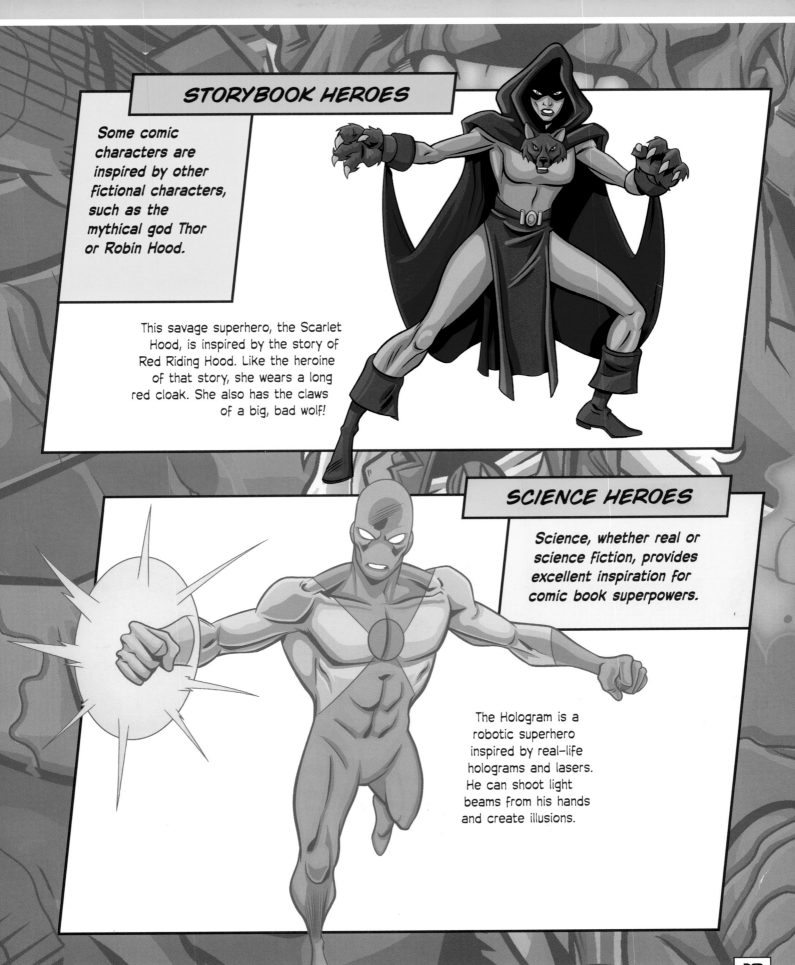

STORYBOOK HEROES

Some comic characters are inspired by other fictional characters, such as the mythical god Thor or Robin Hood.

This savage superhero, the Scarlet Hood, is inspired by the story of Red Riding Hood. Like the heroine of that story, she wears a long red cloak. She also has the claws of a big, bad wolf!

SCIENCE HEROES

Science, whether real or science fiction, provides excellent inspiration for comic book superpowers.

The Hologram is a robotic superhero inspired by real-life holograms and lasers. He can shoot light beams from his hands and create illusions.

THE VULCANOID
FEARSOME FORCE OF NATURE

IT'S TIME TO UNLEASH A SUPERVILLAIN! THE VULCANOID IS INSPIRED BY REAL-LIFE VOLCANOES. HE HAS A ROCKY HIDE AND CAN SHOOT DEADLY BLASTS OF MOLTEN LAVA. HE HAS A HEAVY, BULKY "BRUISER" BUILD AND AN UNUSUAL, ROCKY SKIN TEXTURE.

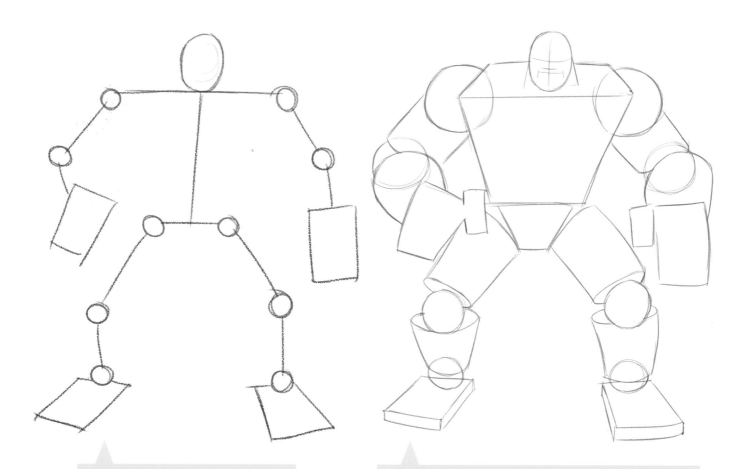

1 Start with an oversized wireframe. Make its head small, but exaggerate the size of its feet and hands.

2 Build on the frame using basic shapes. Begin to fill out the figure, building it up around the shoulders, forearms, and lower legs. Its upper torso should be broad, narrowing at the waist.

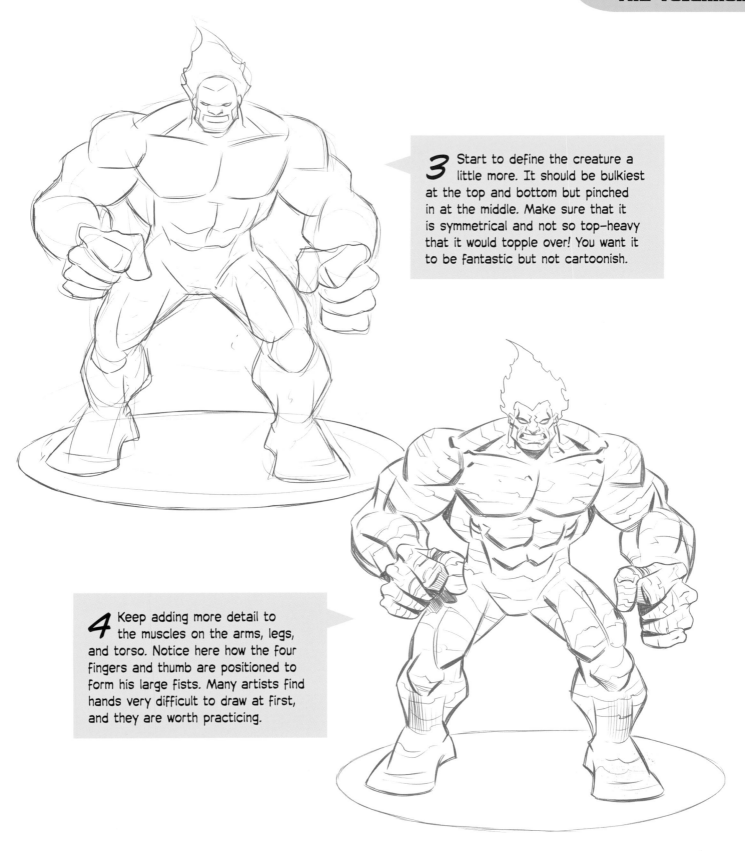

3 Start to define the creature a little more. It should be bulkiest at the top and bottom but pinched in at the middle. Make sure that it is symmetrical and not so top-heavy that it would topple over! You want it to be fantastic but not cartoonish.

4 Keep adding more detail to the muscles on the arms, legs, and torso. Notice here how the four fingers and thumb are positioned to form his large fists. Many artists find hands very difficult to draw at first, and they are worth practicing.

5 Work up the hair, which is flamelike, in keeping with the volcanic theme of the character. It also reminds your reader of the otherworldly, nonhuman traits of this monster. He has no costume since he is a creature of the rocks and earth.

6 The purple hues we have chosen for the Vulcanoid's skin don't look like normal rock, but they are more eye-catching than gray tones. Notice how the molten lava glows through the orange cracks in his skin texture. His hair, eyes, and mouth are all glowing!

ACTION POSES: RUNNING

IN SUPERHERO COMICS, CHARACTERS' MOVEMENTS TEND TO BE LARGER THAN LIFE. READERS WANT TO SEE THEIR HEROES IN CONSTANT ACTION! ARTISTS USE VARIOUS TRICKS TO TAKE A REALISTIC MOVEMENT AND EXAGGERATE IT TO INCREASE ITS VISUAL IMPACT.

REALISTIC RUNNING

When captured in a drawing, realistic running can look surprisingly slow and stately. The limbs of an actual runner swing only so much, and the body is fairly upright.

DYNAMIC RUNNING

In this dynamic image, the character's arms and legs are flung forward and backward, with the body at an extreme angle. The leading hand is very near to us, and the trailing foot seems far away.

ACTION POSES: THROWING A PUNCH

IT WOULD BE RARE FOR A SUPERHERO TO SAVE THE DAY WITHOUT GETTING INTO SOME SORT OF A FIGHT. WHETHER YOU'RE DRAWING A SMALL-SCALE SKIRMISH IN A DARK ALLEY OR A SUPERHUMAN-STRENGTH PUNCH ROCKETING AN ENEMY INTO ORBIT, THE SAME PRINCIPLES APPLY.

REALISTIC PUNCH

A real boxer would be balanced when he throws a punch, keeping his body upright and his feet grounded for maximum stability. But that doesn't look so exciting when you draw it ...

DYNAMIC PUNCH

Instead, a superhero artist relaxes that approach and shifts the body and arms. The punching arm is almost fully extended, while the rear arm is less defensive. Motion lines show power and speed.

AN ACTION SCENE

ONCE YOU HAVE PRACTICED DRAWING YOUR CHARACTERS INDIVIDUALLY IN VARIOUS POSES, TRY PITTING THEM AGAINST EACH OTHER IN A DYNAMIC "SPLASH" PANEL. FOLLOW EACH STEP CAREFULLY, AND THE FINAL IMAGE WILL COME TOGETHER PERFECTLY!

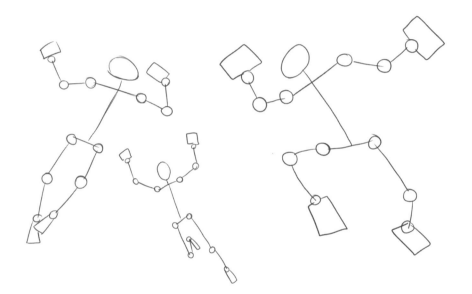

1 Here, three characters are caught up in an aerial battle. The largest character is the hefty Vulcanoid. Victory is smaller than G-Force, because she is farther away from the viewer.

2 The outstretched arms of each of the combatants shows they are balanced and poised, either on the floating platform or in midair, ready to strike. Lightly sketch in the buildings behind them, making sure they look three-dimensional and to scale.

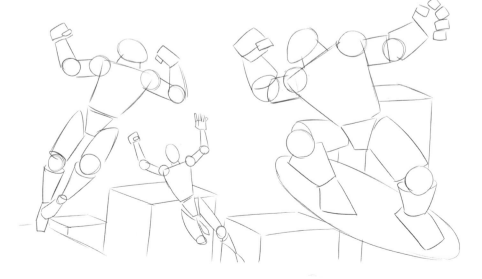

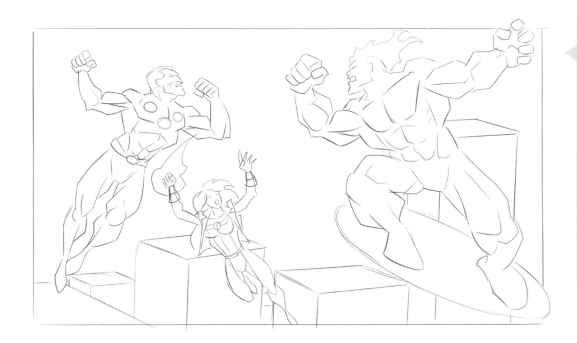

3 Now flesh out each of your characters. Plan the basic positioning of facial features, and sketch in their muscles and costume elements. Where is each character looking? What are they about to do?

4 As you ink the image, pay special attention to your characters' faces. Use a ruler to add details to the buildings. Work in some blocks of shading on G-Force's hair, Victory's costume, and the building behind the Vulcanoid.

5 You might want to practice your coloring in a rough sketch. A mistake on your final artwork could ruin an awful lot of hard work! Keep the background colors light and simple, so that the action leaps off the page.

GLOSSARY

CONSISTENT (kuhn-SIS-tehnt)
Staying the same over time.

DOMINO MASK
(DAH-mih-noh MASK)
A small mask that covers the area around the eyes.

EXAGGERATE (egg-ZAJ-jer-ayt)
To make something larger or more noticeable than it really is.

GUIDE LINE (GYD LYN)
A simple line that shows where to fill in a drawing with more lines or color.

HARD PENCIL (HARD PEN-sill)
A pencil with a hard lead that is good for making thin strokes and fine details in a drawing.

HIGHLIGHTS (HY-lytz)
The brighter parts of an image, which show where light is shining on an object.

INTERACT (in-tuh-RAKT)
To act in a way that affects someone or something else.

MILITARY (MIL-luh-TAYR-ee)
Relating to the army, navy, or air force.

NOIR (NWAHR)
Set in a shadowy setting. Noir stories often feature unhappy characters with confused morals.

PROPORTIONS
(pruh-POHR-shuhnz)
The size of body parts in relation to each other.

ROUGH SKETCH (RUFF SKECH)
A drawing made quickly to give an idea of the finished picture.

SOFT PENCIL (SOHFT PEN-sill)
A pencil with a soft lead that is good for sketching and shading.

WIREFRAME (WYR-fraym)
The basic outline sketch of a character, showing posture and proportion.

FURTHER INFORMATION

WEBSITES

Due to the changing nature of internet links, PowerKids Press has developed an online list of Web sites related to the subject of this book. This site is updated regularly. Please use this link to access the list:

www.powerkidslinks.com/cc/superhero

FURTHER READING

Eisner, Will. *Comics and Sequential Art: Principles and Practices from the Legendary Cartoonist.* New York: W. W. Norton and Company, 2008.

Hiker, Steve. *How to Draw Comic Book Superheroes Using 5 Easy Shapes.* North Charleston, SC: CreateSpace Independent Publishing, 2012.

Lee, Stan. *Stan Lee's How to Draw Comics.* New York: Watson-Guptill Publications, 2010.

McCloud, Scott. *Making Comics: Storytelling Secrets of Comics, Manga and Graphic Novels.* New York: William Morrow Paperbacks, 2006.

Williams, Freddie E. *The DC Comics Guide to Digitally Drawing Comics.* New York: Watson-Guptill Publications, 2009.

INDEX